AWAKENING OF EDEN

The Unwritten Epilogue

AISHANI SWAIN

INDIA · SINGAPORE · MALAYSIA

ISBN
Paperback 979-8-89556-824-8
Hardcase 979-8-89588-996-1

About the Poet

Aishani Swain is a debutant poet with passion for penning poetry with vivid imagery. "*Awakening of Eden: The Unwritten Epilogue*" showcases her unique voice that blends ethereal beauty and sharp realism, by delving into the nuances of human experience including themes of identity, love, and the unseen forces that shape our lives. When she isn't writing, Aishani enjoys listening to and composing music, both of which inspire the rhythmic and melodic qualities in her poetry.

Dedication

To my family, and all readers who sang along to Disney Classic Soundtracks—

May the magic of words bring as much comfort and wonder as those timeless melodies.

Contents

Withered Salvation

Once the petal falls
It's the final straw

To the game we were born to play
Will the heavens cry at your fallen grace

A passing breeze isn't considered
In a world of trees
Will you crawl your way out
Wait to be noticed
Forgetting to notice
Cry until you bleed
Beg to not be forgiven

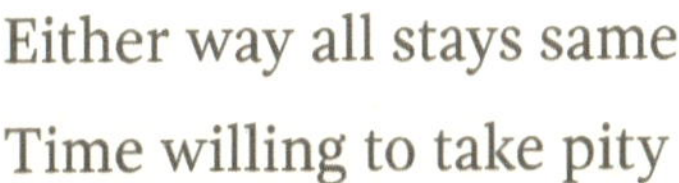

Either way all stays same
Time willing to take pity

Foes cast upon your tainted friendships
All you end up doing
Is bathe in their deceit
Pluck your feathers
Until none is left but one

A difference unnoticed
Caught, in a trap as you may

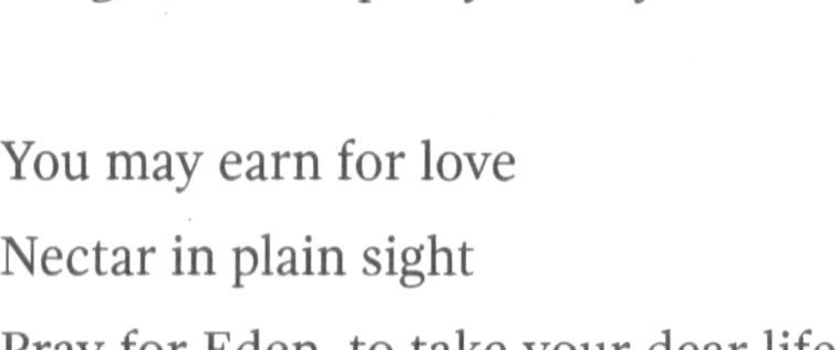

You may earn for love
Nectar in plain sight
Pray for Eden, to take your dear life

Never After

Would the ocean stay silent
At the breath of your eyes
Every moment spent in your presence
Is a gift bestowed upon

Why do you cry my dear?
When the whole world stops
To glance your perfect valour

Of all I have met
Only you have caught my eye

It saddens me
Knowing I won't have the same space
In your heart

One day, you will come to realise

Or will I

This was a sentence

in the facade of a fairy tale

Where the villain always meets
the tragic end

Yet Happily Ever After is
impossible to obtain

As the story unfolds

So will the hidden chances

If the heavens were to take my side

Adhere to my faith

One look from your eyes

Yearning for your devotion

Is all I live for

Touch of Time

Be willing to grace the sword
When time withers
It glazes your back
For your finest hour

Kneel before those beneath you
Rise to protect
The ones who loved you

Have the faith
To believe for the forsaken

Days Carry on
To never look back

On those who lack

Pointless pleas are regardless

Virtues practiced by

Live on

Will your saviour be the one by your side

Or the meek feathers

Who stayed by you

Oppressed by your thoughtless views

Breathe

Look at the sky once in a while,
it carries the memories of those

who once walked the earth
and those who will.

Daylight

Drops of the sun bloom,
awakening the morning glum.
Shine bright as day passes through.

You're the sunshine
That makes each day worthwhile

Sunlit Hues

Hazel brown bursts of warmth
Wrap around your endearing love

Dynamic as you are
Feisty as you tend to be
One smile sends to haven
Only unlocked by you

I would move the stars
Just to be with you

Your maternal love compares
To none of the feeling felt before

May you be blissful
Through every moment
As two guardians and a knight
Will keep you happy every step of the way
Always will I love you, is no doubt
My allegiance to you is
out of respect and grace
As you deserve the most
A day no significant than other

Yet today was the day an angel
Graced me with love and life

Princess

Who will listen to my pleas
When your tears hold no meaning

Yet my voice yearns
to be heard by your heart

Waiting by the window
Time fails to pass me by

Only the faint footsteps
Of what used to be
Echos the barren halls
Where you and I
Were the ones sharing the memories
Of our dear ones

You were the ending that I need
To my fairytale

I was just the minute fault in a line
Noticed, just to be erased

Remnants left behind
Is the husk I dreamed to be
One piece at a time
A part of me changed
Forever faulted

Desperate for a new beginning

Scorned Legacy

We bathe in the sins of our ancestors
While they rest in peace

Where does the future lie?
When we beg for forgiveness

Futures written; the moment eyes awaken
Slight drift, right tale is forsaken
Truths are lies with evidence
Yet those without proof
Cry wolf, in vain

Will you listen, while they bleed tears?
Or wait for the moment

They stop crawling for hope

Every day is a mystery we walk into
Yet we turn a blind eye to taking risks

We share our emotions
Expecting to be heard

Why not listen to the person
Who calls out to you everyday

Help yourself first
Survive to help others

Expectations

May the sorrows of your past
Still stay beside you

As you await for time
For them to change you

Every word pricks like a needle
A single drop of fails to awaken you

Will the piercing glances hurt more?
The fear of the unknown will strike first
Blocking out your thoughts won't help

It cripples you from within
Giving no chance of forgiving

Classics retain
Good triumphs evil
While facing evil everyday
Letting it win
Winning all wars is a predicament

Try all you want

In the end, you will be scrapping for hope
At the bottom of the well

Blessing

Silent notes
Written in a moment of desperation
Was it truly you who passed my mind

People never last forever
Their memories carry on

You were the story that I never forgot
Each tune of your voice
had a melody of its own
A song meant to be heard
By the longest of souls

In the darkness I found
my companion
While my light dimmed away

A mistake might have been the greatest
choice ever made

The answer couldn't be defined
In two words

While you stole my words away
Knitting a destiny of your own

Blossom

Over a thousand buds,
only one blooms.

The survival of the fittest,
the kindest ones wither the first.

The chance only occurs once,
it's your choice if you wish to use it.

Riverside

Swimming without a worry as the world carries on,
oblivious to the words spoken to us.

I will find my way back to you
no matter how far the tides separate us.

Symphony of Change: A Beloved Grace

Blessed I was, to bloom with angels
With Wings reaching for the stars
Yet all those around me shone bit brighter

Natural it shall be
The favorite is most certainly me

Why is it, I am being shut out
When it's certainly supposed to be me

Stuck in a little girl 's ploy
Tainted by your actions
That broke us farther apart
Cruel shots of guilt, shadowed over me

Only to realize
My heart played me like a child's game
Rationality having a turf with one's desires
In the end, it was our greatest hopes
Moulding our future together
In our small unity, resolute and sound,
A crack, though small, fate's bond surrounds
With poise and grace, I longed to live

An artist's stroke spoke forbidden words
Feelings painted over and over again
Failing to convey, the words
concealing the artist

Earning to be the shooting star I
need to be
Aphrodite 's gift blossomed over the
years
So grew the valour to confront yesteryear's tide,
As strength embraced the echoes, where emotions
abide

But in matters of love, there can be no pretense, no artífice

Though your heart belongs to another
I was my own, second to none
Neither will I be yours

If the heavens were to take pity,
I pray you may find it in your heart
to return my affection
As I found peace moving on,
From what could have been

Awe

A sight only to be seen once,
bathe in its beauty or swallow it as one.

Eternal beauty only lasts once,
the moment it's fades, forgotten like no other.

Gem

Various shades of emerald
adorn our earth.

Yet they are robbed
from a future they deserve.

Each dew-drop rests on its leaves.
A home found its place.

L'esprit De L'esalier

Shards of glass never bleed
Yet the look on your face is everlasting
Thousands of words could have been spoken
Not one uttered a word
Waiting for the inevitable chance
That would never occur

Could a shatter have made a difference?
Or just an insignificant ripple in time
Forgotten like the dews of the past

I was the shackles in your daring life
That pierced your every dream
While I drowned endlessly in mine
Hoping to find the "*Happily Ever After*»
In this cruel fairy tale

As words ran out

So did our time

Would I find you in the place I left you?

Hoping you would be gone

Yet, when I am welcomed by
the silent breeze

A part of me is missing

Longing for your lost presence

Following the fool's whispers

I search tirelessly

Only to meet my destined fate

Living the life, we dreamed of together

With another

Star crossed

Farther apart we go
Even if our eyes meet
Vast seas embark on a journey
With a never-ending story

Words spoken before
Are merely a daydream now

Missing those times won't help
As they have moved on
Similarities at first
Differed in our hearts

One dreamt of loving
While the other lived

Star crossed lovers
Collided across the skies

Perhaps the opposite ends were never supposed to meet

Holding onto the last branch
May or may not help
One tried to keep hoping for a change

While the other had changed
Beyond recognition

Empty promises

Separated by hues,
held by the tears through the skies.

As the night falls
the daylight embraces its escape.

Chance

Taking a step
Always shatters a heart

May it break the ice
Leaving back the past
Is a heart wrenching choice
Memories of the good times
Forgets the mistakes

Both played a role
In shaping your life
The audience may share your demise
Only you know
what went behind the curtains

Shameful pasts are not a reason to hide
To people you shall never meet
It's a gift to your future

Facing it, is an understatement
Make the person proud
Who looked up to you
Hoping to live as the *better you*

Achieve

As sword is better than a pen
A bud can't fathom to a flower
All bloom in the early spring
So why didn't I?

The blooming ones look at me with pity
While I wither away with the winter snow

Getting back up is the easy part
Staying on track challenges us all

The one I got from the shining star
Feared me the most
Knowing I would never reach as high
As the world was in the sky
It was in his eyes

More and more I try not too much
I know that I have been in their minds

Feelings that won't leave no matter what
Haunt me like a wailing spirit
To shed my scales and thoughts
Is the only way of escape

To the world I am not sure how I am
I shall begin with an identity
That is accepted by myself first

Timeless Love

No boundaries exist for my feeling
An arrow would be a feather
If it meant to be your shield
Hurtful as it may, your love is all I need

Starting out a feeling unknown
Blossomed into a flower
Ever so delicate by your touch
Shattering at your absence

In circles we go, in a everlasting loop
Our conversations repeat
Through and through

Your blood, sweat and tears will be
Acknowledged by prophets

Even if that prophet may just be
A sweet little lad

A small scruple makes no difference
My feelings will remain unchanged
Looking for ways to stretch even a second
Desperate as it may be, so is forgetting
Time will pass on, so will our memories

Our moments together
Will forever be embedded into symphonies

Lover of beauty

As the last snow reaches the ground
Time stops as if no one is around
A moment frozen just for us
Yet all our eyes do is interlock

Silence greets us like an old friend
Do you think we will ever escape?

A second can be stretched
into a thousand chances
One of them might be enough
To let my feelings blossom
Taking care of it is the hard part
Let it wither away
Earning for nurture

Love is cruel to the point
Our feelings will always flicker

Do you think we stand a chance
Against the rules of nature?

Beauty fades, so will I
Will I be loved when there is nothing left
I will work hard to the point my hands bleed
Only for you to step on my dreams
A point will occur
when we have none but us
Soon it will be you and I who will be against each other

My rustic heart drowns
in your endearing love
Only time will tell
if I get destroyed or saved first

Strings of fate

As morning dew drops embrace the sun
Your smile brightens the darkest corners
Caring as they come
Loving as you are, it's more than luck
That I ended up with you

Home is a place in your embrace
Never wanting to leave you side
Is an understatement

I'm sure of your faith in me
Will make you think of me always

Times will continue to pass us by
No matter to my dislike

Yet each moment spent will be special
Till the story ends

Remember me when the stars cover the night sky
I will remember the moon shining graciously above

We were meant to be together
As our stories were intertwined
From the beginning of time

Magic spell

The spell's about to wear off
As the dreadful hour nears
The lies waiting for a chance to escape
The shallow truth begs to stay

Never felt so alive in this dreadful facade
Yet the reality is sharper than a bullet
I'm afraid to admit that the world has changed
It is I who the world is afraid to face

History writes what fits the story
What about the supporting character who gave it her all?
As the lead actress finishes as final scene
The audience showers with applause
Waiting for the moment she breaks down

Over and over the same role continues
As the final curtain call occurs
The actress dances her last dance
With a shed of tear

As the audience is no longer
Interested in her washed up performance

The wait

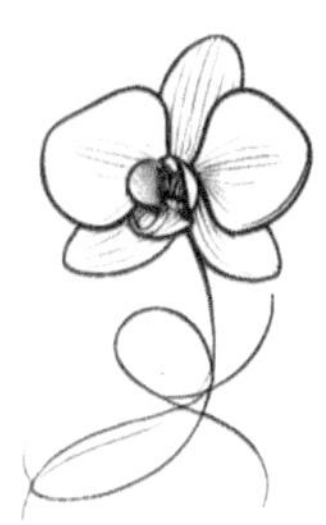

Deeper than the ocean
Faster than the wave
would words be able to express
how I always feel about you?

Fall of the raindrops
Pass by every second
Waiting your reply
While you wait for someone else
Oblivious to the known

Begging for the lie
I knew from the begging

Yet my feelings shielded me
My heart earns to wait for you more
Will that be enough?

Neither one will change
As we are caught in this endless loop
Of neither love nor fate

True Love

The purest form of love
is that where you love unconditionally.

It can save or destroy you,
as you discover the ethereal abyss.

Fate

Beauty is a curse
That fools all, but one

The holder has the burden to know it all
Happiness cannot be lost
Until the very end
Hope is the key in this lost world

To trust you was a mistake
As your clouded judgement affected mine
The steps we took was a faux from the very beginning

Uncanny events brought us together
Yet it's a blessing that I can see the true you

Would things be the same if my mouth was locked away?

As you would prefer a doll who said nothing anyway

The truth will be out of your mind

Yet your lies are all I see

Eyes covered with the light of the person I prayed for

Slowly fading away

As my nightmare take over

For as many memories await us

We can only dream about this day

Where we both earn our freedom

As all hope is not lost, until I cut the last string

Wish

A silent voice heard
through a thousand cries
Yet the outcome doesn't change
No matter how hard I try

Pins and needless
Sharp as they maybe
Blunt to the words
Uttered by yours, truly

Nameless deities prayed upon
Fruitless boons wished, bestowed
Together we are counted as one

Yet our efforts are equivalent to none
Never again, will I think of giving up

Admitting defeat is not something
I was made for

Hope is always around the corner
I just have to try my best
To find its deepest desires

Lonesome Friend

Calm as the waves, still the water goes.

Let it wash away your fears,
As the lonesome tear sheds
to be your only companion.

Prince charming

Once there was a prince
Who was loved all throughout the land
Except by the *one* who loathed him

Every passing day
All hard attempts were futile
The hater's mind was set in stone

The red string of fate ends
at the heart of the castle

The prince could find his yours truly
Afraid of the person before him

Harsh and Sharp, the words thrown
Hurt the prince

Soon all over the land people knew
How cowardly their king would be
Hidden in the reflection,
the animal laughed

His predictions came true
No matter what

Pride

Know for sure, that I will best you in every way
As I am the sharpest tool ever made

Help is a word never sought after
Who needs it?
For it is I,
Foes cower at my sight

Freedom

Freedom to those who can’t ask
Freedom to those who can’t fight back

A voice failed to be heard
While a thousand wail in return
Shunned for uttering the truth
The lies are reality we endure

Better or worse is not something we want
To be an equal is what we deserve

Freedom is a right not a privilege
Yet the colour of our skin
Determined our worth

Rules are worthless if they are beneficial
Shackles on your own breed
Makes you worse than any animal

Pushed to the point of no turning back
You're the one to blame
Our raging war smithering your prison

Waves

The ocean shore shimmering with a high breeze
A moment to be frozen in time indeed
The sea of glaciers eventually disappears
Overpowering the people that hurt her

The tears flowing though the cities lived
Consuming one livid soul at a time
Years to come this will follow
Eventually all that will be left is her shadow

The world is going on a journey
I'm not ready to see

Soon our fates will meet
Despite our best interference

All efforts are fruitless now
The time's up, we have to face the clock

One may defeat all odds
Without anyone present, all hope is lost

As the sand still continues to fall
A chance is gifted
Use it to your most convenience
It won't come again

Sun kissed

Warmth of joy, surrounds you always.

Find the key that opens the window to
explore the world beyond.

Experience life, to it's full potential.

Lilac

Tainted words disguised as a treat
While you spoke words that provoked me
Wishing for those lost feelings was a waste
When I could have hoped for serenity instead

My wish did come true
In the most unexpected way
I couldn't be happier
Than any other day to come

Hand in hand promises were made
Broken as easily as glass breaks

There is no use crying over the fallen
As peace is before you, over it's démise

This moment was silently prayed upon
By two hearts never meant to be together
Forged together through unstable emotions
It was bound to happen soon enough
The smiles won't be forgotten
Neither will the tears

Two fighters won't win a war
One wasn't willing to step down
The other forced to

Youth

Memories fade so will we
Our talks have turned into scripts
As we reminisce our times together
We forget our lines here

Will we ever get our lost time?
Upon fate's cruel heart, it lies
Hoping our cries to be heard
In vain we let go of our promises

We let hope slip past our hearts
We beg for chances like withering roses
Beauty wilts and so will we

Our choices are faded with emotion
Unclear and vast like the horizon waiting

All that is left now is waiting endlessly
Until the hourglass let's go of it's final tear
We would be reunited as the heavens rejoice
As the greatest war would have ended
At the hands of its fragile warriors

Envy

All it takes is a drop for the hourglass to start
As the desire grow larger within time
For all I want, shall be mine

One grain at a time is precious to all
Those snickering faces
Feeding of the same poisonous vine
As they enamour themselves
With class and dignity
That I can never achieve

A life just out of reach
What makes them so different from me?
Born and made of blood that worked tirelessly
Feeding off their power and greed

String of Plays

Each thread carries a story,
Each vein carries the strength to sustain you.

Once cut, the whole narration falls apart
The stage and the actors are remnants of the unforgiving past.

Greed

Ivory pearls and the gold champagne
May not distract you from their snickers
The alluring scent of schemes for sure
Has the space to stab your back

One may have a lot but the other just wants more
There is never enough
Too much may fill it to the brim
One more drop
Everything will spill

Friendships more fragile than glass
Yet the eye for the forbidden fruit
Is stronger than any diamond found

"Why does he have it?"

"I can have more If want to"

Bargaining words of a sinner

To justify their tainted actions

Is worth no less than a penny to the well healed

Hiding behind the facade of hard work and determination

It has fooled and grown to con us all

Feeding on the fears of being less worthy

Forever locked in a everlasting game

A gamble of having or losing it all

Oath

To love and to protect I shall
A vow I am forsaken to have
Thou simple wish of mine
Is solely for you to shine

The thought of you washing it all away
A fear cripples me
I simply cannot adhere
The decision is yours to make my dear

Yet the trigger waiting for you
A friend or a foe
Will always be present

No matter how hard you try
It will never disappear

The constant urge to intervene
Is barricaded by the thoughts of losing you
Only if you would just listen
Oh, how much I can help you so

A drop won't make a difference
It will just tip the flow just a little

Soon you shall realise
It was all for you
An oath I took, unbreakable

For you shall never be free
From the love that will poison you
Over and over again

Haven

Beneath the blanket of stars
Was the moon that I cherish the most
Countless moments spent with you
Would replay in my record player
As I cherished the words we shared

Though the tides were often rough
It calmed, as we saw the best in each other

Being with me at my happiest times
Made me to always think of you
Being with me through my worst
Made me never forget you

Your laugh is the serotonin, that makes my day
Oh Darling, I can never forget our bickering and conversations

I keep trinkets of those memories
As those were the happiest times
That I can remember Far apart, we might be
However, it doesn't differ my feeling for you
It only keeps increasing as the days pass by

Uncertainty is the challenge we face
But I want my possibilities to be with you

If so, heaven exists,
I would love to spend as many of my days with you
Cause I found the haven,
where I needed to be

Just saying "I love you" isn't enough for me
You mean more to me that those three words can ever adhere

Hireath

Longing for a place that was never mine
I still can't find it no matter how hard I try

Comforted by an embrace that was never there
The smell of old books fills the air

Each step feels like I am walking on a cloud
My childhood innocence has just been found
Memories shared could all be a lie
I still can't abide to the truth in-front of my eyes

As the clouds fade away
The smell of books goes away
All that's left, is pitch black
Consumed by shadows of false hope

Alluring Trance

As you walk by the crowd
My eyes only see you

As your alluring scent fills the room
Rhythms drumming to the beat of your steps
the violin played it's last song
I can only hear your voice
like a poisonous trance

Gamble

A hidden secret
Exposed at every moment
Every choice we ever make
Has a chance to go wrong

We are hopeful, it's the other half for sure
A new lover, friend or foe
Looks aren't always deceiving
Often, they are true to their nature

Hiding behind the strong upfront
Won't help hide the cowardice for long
Fear always catches up
It's rotten half we can't get rid of

Addicted to the rush we can't help
Hypocrites enjoy it more than they say
One wrong move and everything goes downwards

That's what makes life intriguing
Don't you think so?

Hues of Blue

A rare sapphire is inside you
You shine brighter than the blue hues around you
No matter how fierce the tides are
Never give up the shining hope you bare

As warm their words may seem
Their icy intents can be seen right through
A truth always has a lie hidden
Can I find out what's within?

As a clear sky you still keep a happy façade
Can you keep doing that all day?

As the '*Devil's hour*' appears
Will your happy smiles disappear?

As my façade comes to an end
Will you finally show your true face?

The mysteries that lie beneath the ocean
Will soon be revealed
Peoples' deepest fears
will come out from within

Invidia

In the coldest winter
The wind blows
Covering the truth from my eyes

As rain pours from the sky
My heart buried under the snow
Waiting for me to reveal
The evil that is bound to show

It's feeds from your own flaws
Stuck in this dark abyss
You're bound to break
There nothing you can do
As it has already taken over you

Even the happiest memories can't save you
As you are a prey to this deadly hound

Giving up is the best choice
But even that won't work
All you can do is resist the throes
of anticipation

Ataraxia

The days go by
As the breeze follows my way
The world is frozen with silence
As I watch the streams dancing away
The rain pours all day
As I watch time pass away
It's so blissful, I could just ponder all day

I wonder what's going on
Outside my very jolly little cage
The rain starts to slow
The breeze flows away
I wonder what else will go away.

The stream calms down
As if all the joy is taken out

Time now continues

In its mocking way

Waiting for me to realise

That the world doesn't work my way.

Honey Dew

The rays of warmth
bathe the sun awaiting the dewy eyes.

The day always starts,
setting your eyes on your fated soulmate

Warm Winters

Spring came,

awaiting the summer storm.

Each petal holding a memory and happiness of our snowy past.

Desiderium

Eternity goes by
And I still miss your eyes
I waited for you day and night
But you were nowhere in sight

My memory starts to fade
As I remember our old days
Hope is a strong word
But it disappears like it wants you gone

Tears fall down my eyes
But I don't know why
The world goes on
Like nothing ever happened

But I am stuck in the abyss

With doubts and disappointment

Whatever I do will not bring you back

I don't even know, if we were destined to this nightmare

Retribution

Priceless crystal drops
As bright as the sky
Prays for my restorations
While the souls whisper

My hands tied
With the allure of
My own nature
Never did I realise
How fast the time has passed by

My hourglass ended
So did my days

Condemning as it may
A chance to change, I plead

Even if it's the greatest betrayal

To my fallen self

Bright as the moonlight was

It reflects a persona

We were never the same

One prayed to, one prayed for

Hidden Protectors

Eyes of all follow us around,
the most unexpected watch over you.

Protecting you,
whenever and wherever.

Pillar of Virtue

A work spoken
Holds a thousand emotions
Yet the courage to speak
Halts at the glimpse of your tears

Would you be willing to take my hand?
As it may comfort
Or be the one you use to climb up with me
A shoulder always there for you

Tricks of Time

Each step you take
Is always elegant
But the beauty that lies beneath
Is priceless

As time passes by
We wait to be together
Is fate so cruel
That we can't see each other?

At the crucial moment
Hoping for the right moment
Is hopeless
Bound to this curse
Of the cruel fate

Now all we can do is pass the blame

But in the end we all know

It's our instincts

That drove us to the end

To this unforgivable deed

A Momentary Occurrence

Owning every moment that occurs
The occurrence to live
By my own ticking clock
Is a dream that falters

Sandcastles by the beach
Every turquoise hues
Caresses the breeze
By the peace of my mind
Together we shall pass
In honour of the future
Yet an impasse occurs

We are left in different points in time
Forgotten vows
False promises

Yet, all I can remember
Is the peace of mind
We used to share
Are we bounds by Freedom
To realise, the illusion of peace
Was just a momentary epiphany
An anecdote, waiting to be remembered

King of the Ocean

The beasts of the seas
Bow to none but one
Too big to fit in,
Your heart shrunken to the depth of your desire

Feared by all, I embody their fear, as do they

Crashing waves in a spectacle
The moment the castle falls crumbling, joys echo the water
The mighty beast has fallen, leaving all satisfied
All continues, as it goes on
Another will soon take its place

The power of the beast is the loneliest of all
Will sympathy be shed when it passes?

Will it's companions mourn a loss?

Abandoned, leaving all content, awaiting for the next chapter in its fateful tale

www.ingramcontent.com/pod-product-compliance
Lightning Source LLC
LaVergne TN
LVHW041120150826
845673LV00007B/2140

* 9 7 9 8 8 9 5 5 6 8 2 4 8 *